First Stories

My Friend P

by Altan

Macdonald

In the sea there is an iceberg.

On the iceberg is a penguin.
He's my friend.

He has a hat
to keep his head warm.

He has skating boots
to keep his feet warm.

. . . and so he can skate
FAST on the ice.

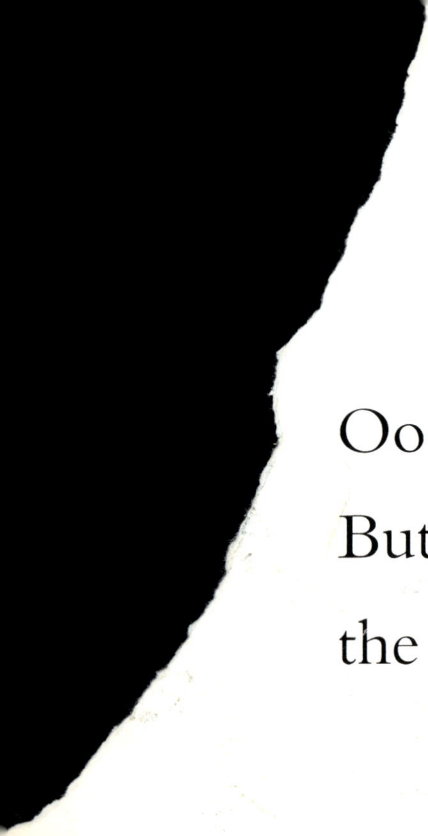

Ooops!
But when he slips
the ice is cold.

Now he wants his gloves.

Poor penguin!
He needs hat and skates
AND gloves outside.

But inside
his house of ice

the water in the bath is warm.

Now he doesn't need
any clothes at all!

Afterwards

he puts on a dressing-gown

and goes to bed
warm as toast.

Concept and illustrations by Francesco Tullio-Altan
English text by Helen East

First published 1986 by
La Editoriale Libraria S.p.A. Trieste, Italy
This edition published 1986 by
Macdonald & Co (Publishers) Ltd
Greater London House
Hampstead Road
London NW1 7QX

ISBN 0 356 11810 X

Made and printed in Italy by
La Editoriale Libraria S.p.A. Trieste